DATE DUE

APR 2 6 1989			
MAY 2 3 1989			
OCT 1 6 1989			
NOV 1 6 1989			
SE 24 '90			
OCT 1 1 '90			

599.61
Moo

Moon, Cliff
Elephants in the wild

Upsala Area Schools
ELEMENTARY LIBRARY
Upsala, MN 56384

Elephants in the wild

Cliff Moon

Wayland

In the Wild

Elephants in the Wild
Lions in the Wild

Further titles are in preparation

This book is based on an original text by Edmund Rogers.

First published in 1984 by
Wayland (Publishers) Ltd
49 Lansdowne Place, Hove
East Sussex BN3 1HF, England

© Copyright 1984 Wayland (Publishers) Ltd

ISBN 0 85078 373 9

Phototypeset by
Kalligraphics Ltd, Redhill, Surrey
Printed in Italy by
G. Canale & C.S.p.A., Turin
Bound in the UK by
The Pitman Press, Bath

Contents

Elephants	5
Food for Elephants	11
Elephants' Lives	21
At the Water-hole	31
Moving On	41
Answers to Questions	54
Index	56

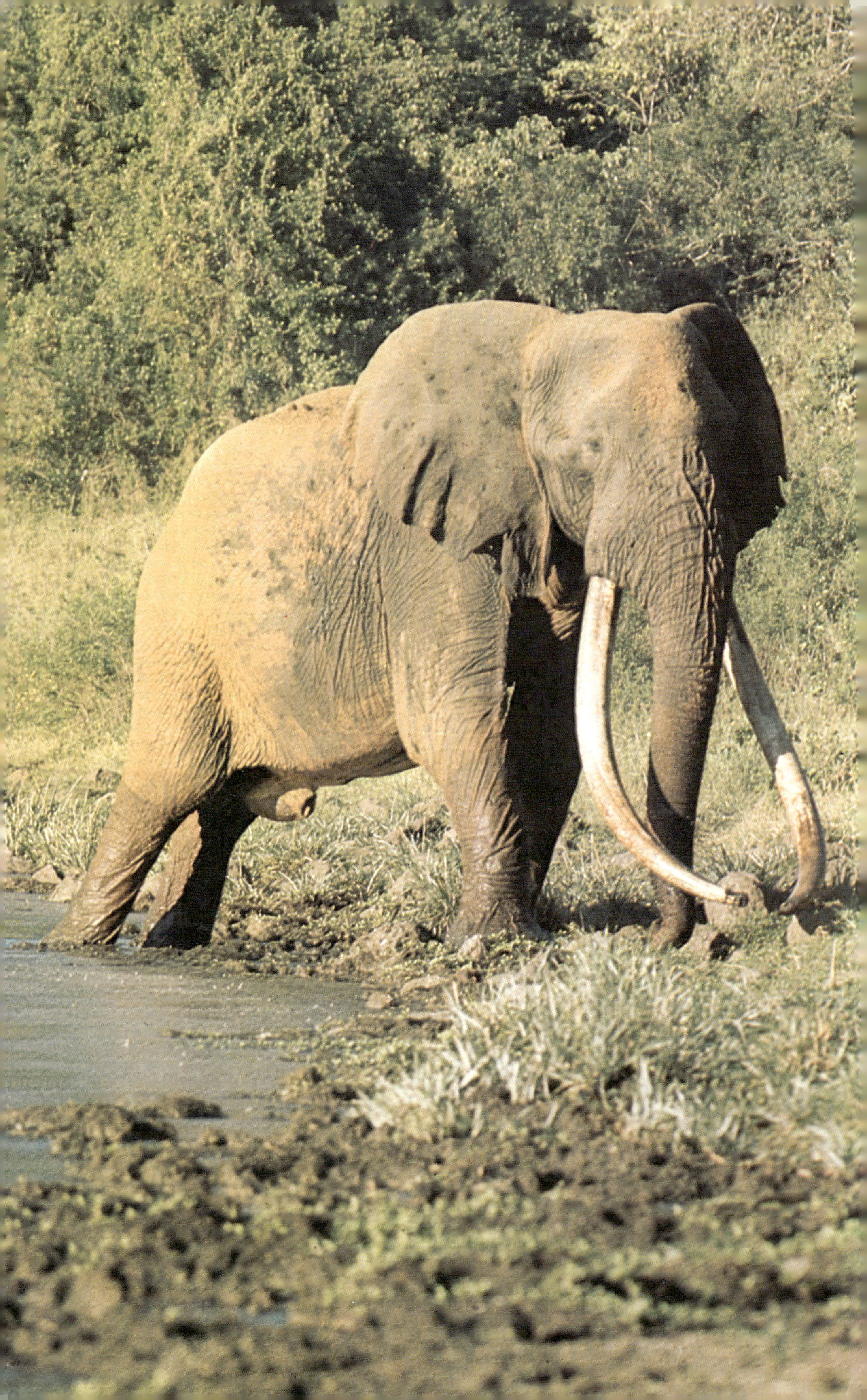

Elephants

How big is an elephant?
Bigger than you,
bigger than a horse and
bigger than a hippo!
Elephants are the biggest animals
that live on land.

This elephant is called Ahmed.
He is an African elephant and
he weighs about 6 tonnes (6 tons).
He has very long tusks
that touch the ground and
they weigh 25 kg (55 lb) each.

This elephant is fully grown.
His tusks started growing
when he was 2 or 3 years old.

Elephant tusks are made of ivory.
Really they are teeth
that kept on growing.

Look at this elephant's eye.
It is very small and
the long eyelashes
help to shade it
from the sun.
Elephants can only see
for about 50 metres (55 yards).

Elephants work hard in India.
They are taught how to carry
heavy loads.
Sometimes they pull logs and
sometimes they lift things
with their trunks.
Elephants are easy to train
because they have large brains
and good memories.

This Indian elephant
has been trained to work
on the farm.

Elephants have very thick skins.
Can you think why?
(Answer on page 54)

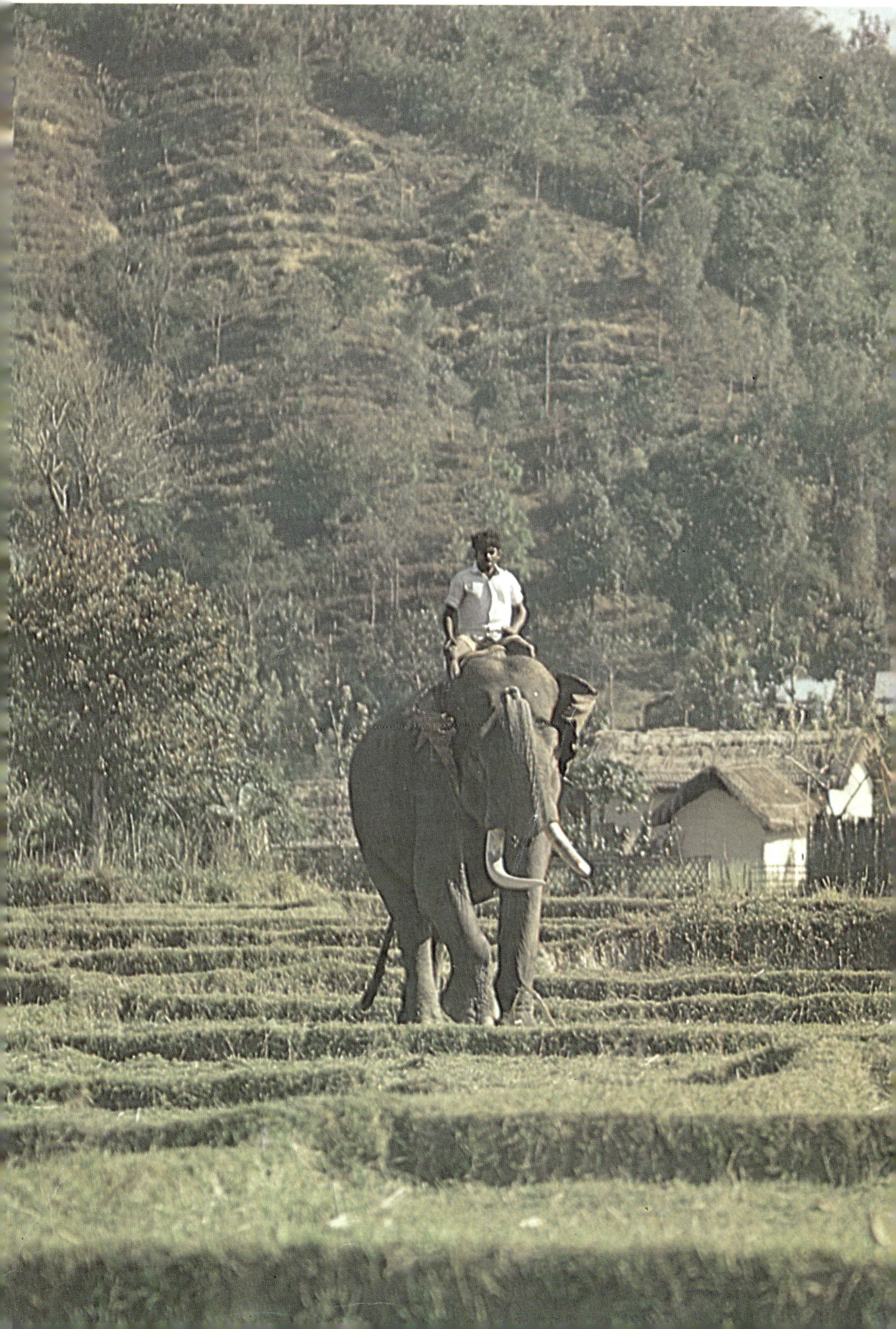

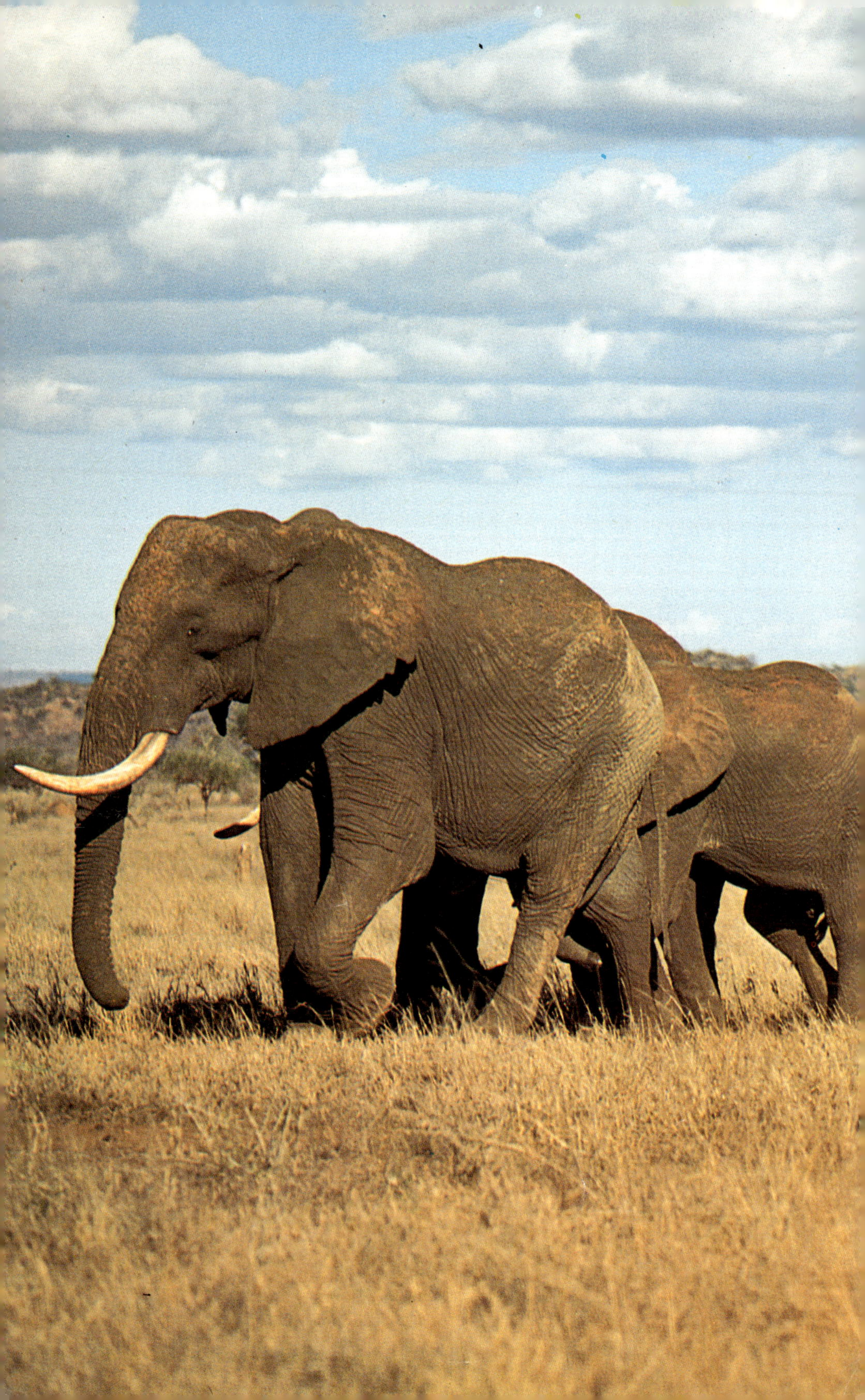

Food for Elephants

These are African elephants
living wild in the bush.
They stay together in a **herd**
so that they can look after
each other.

It is early morning and
the elephants are drinking
from the river.
They eat berries, roots,
tree bark and grass.

Elephants like eating tree bark
because it is very tasty.
These elephants are tearing
the bark off the trees
with their tusks and
putting it in their mouths
with their trunks.
Sometimes they stretch their trunks
up into the trees to pick leaves.

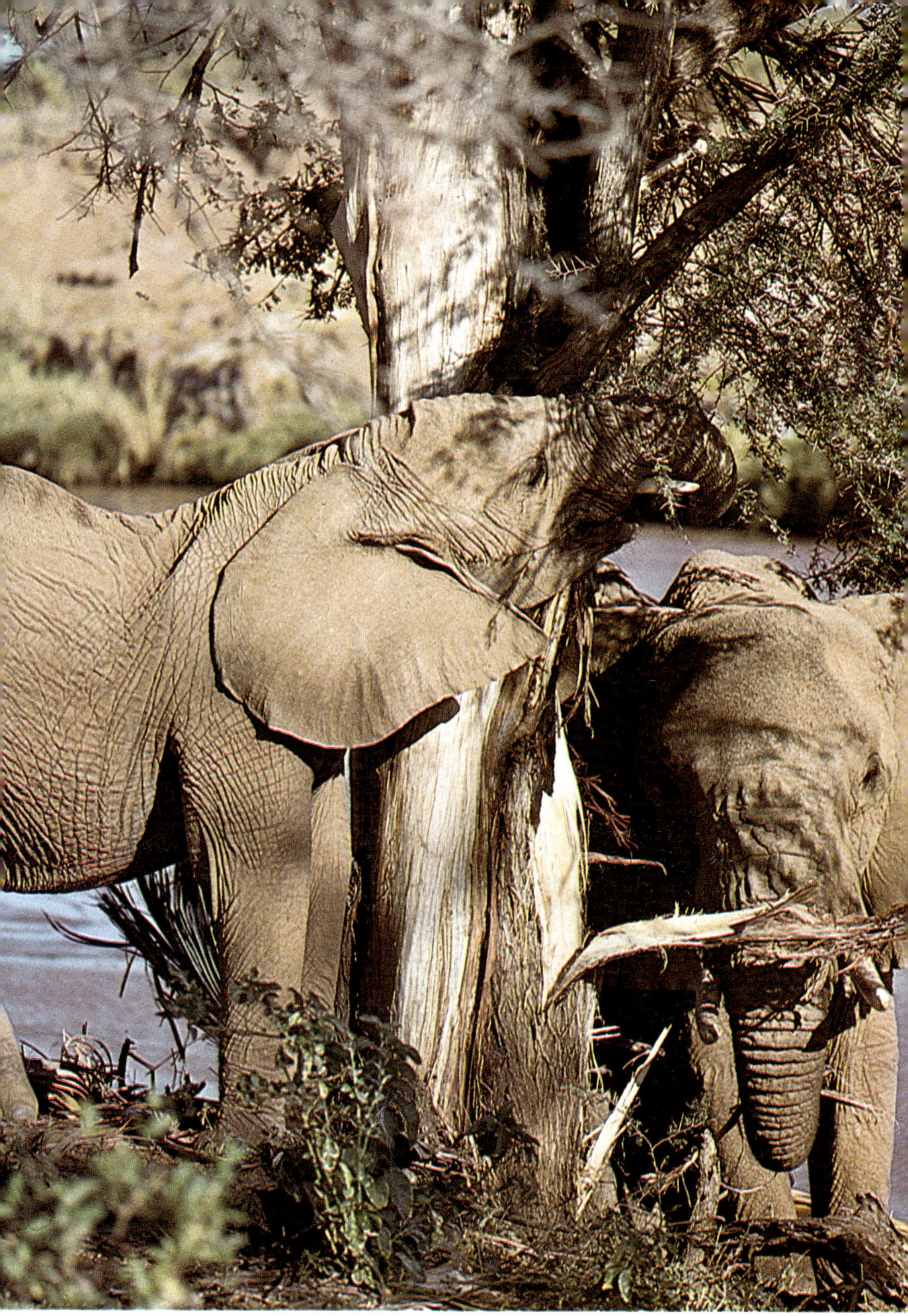

This is what happens to tasty trees
when elephants come along!
There are 50 to 100 elephants
in a herd so lots of trees
end up like this.

The elephants have moved on.
This is what the trees and ground
look like after they have finished
eating their meal.

But why do you think the elephants
have moved on?
(Answer on page 54)

17

Elephants that live in zoos
eat buns and sandwiches.
This African elephant doesn't live
in a zoo but she likes picnics!
You can see why she is called
'Dustbin Nellie'!

If you look for droppings and footprints you can see where elephants have been. When it rains the droppings get washed into the ground to help new plants to grow. Then there will be fresh food for the elephants to eat.

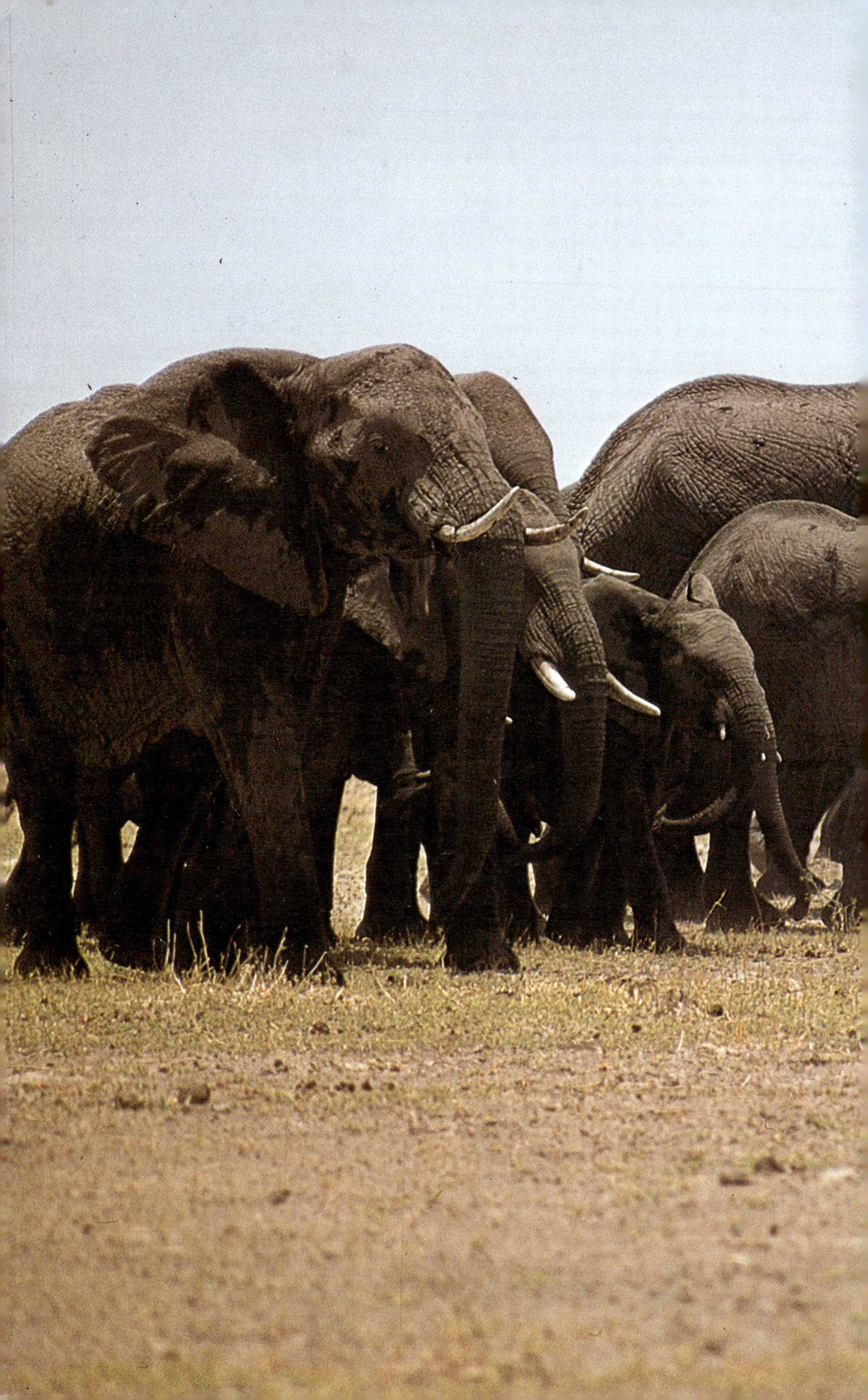

Elephants' Lives

Male elephants are called **bulls** and females are called **cows**. The bull will mate with the cow and later she may have a baby elephant.

Sometimes two bulls fight
with their tusks.
If a tusk breaks near the tip
it will grow again.

A bull mated with this cow and now she has had a baby. Her baby grew inside her for 22 months.

The baby elephant sucks milk from its mother for 2 or 3 years. Then it starts to eat grass, leaves and plants.

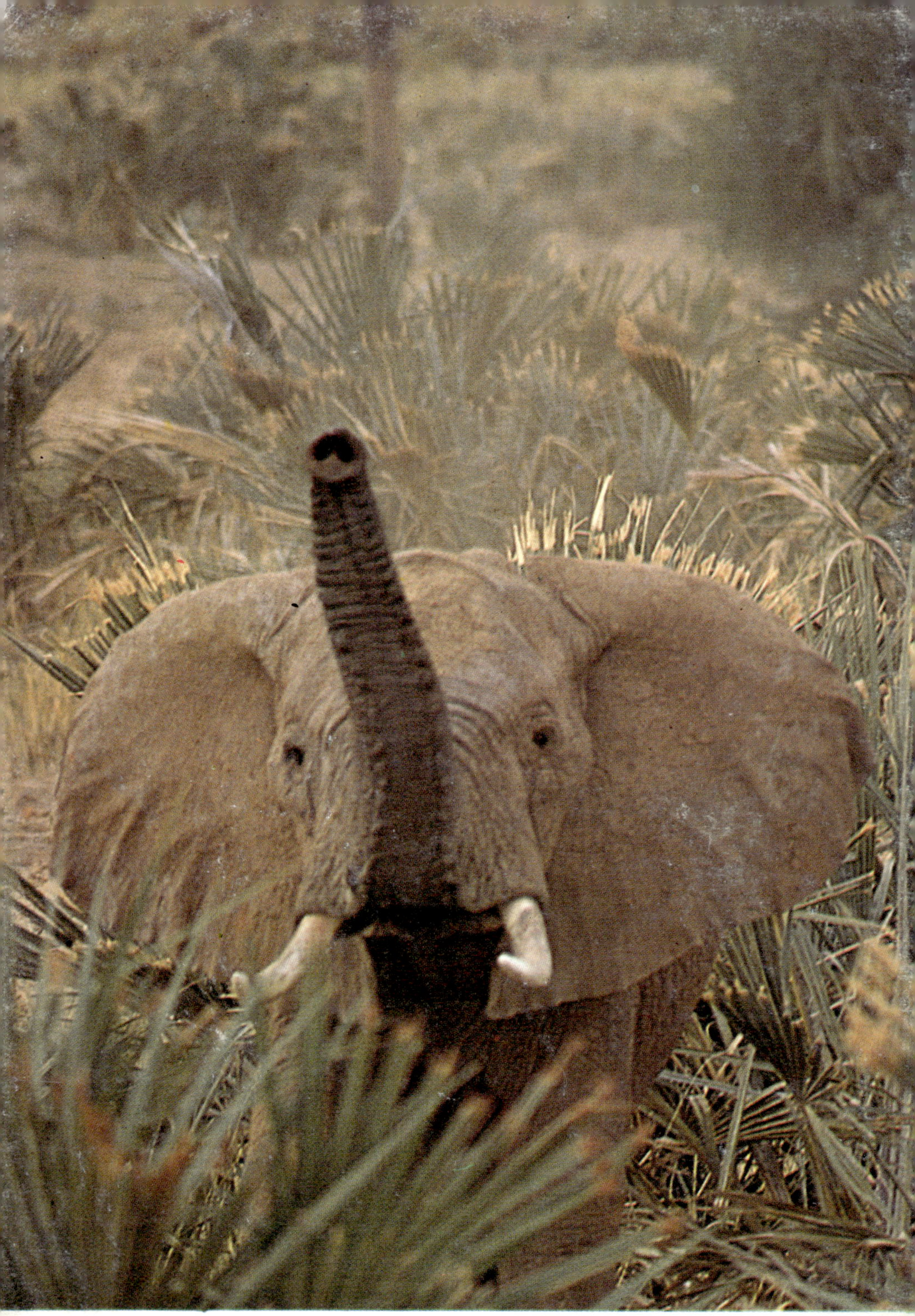

Look at the elephants' trunks.
Their trunks are really big noses.

What can this elephant smell?
It might be something to eat
or it might be a lion coming
to attack the baby elephants.

Elephants don't like lions
or tigers because sometimes
they attack their babies.
When a lion or tiger comes near
all the big elephants start to
flap their ears and trumpet loudly.
Then the whole herd charges
to frighten the enemy away.

These birds live with the elephants.
If a lion comes near
the birds fly up in the air
and that warns the elephants.
But the birds do something else
for the elephants.
Can you think what it is?
(Answer on page 54)

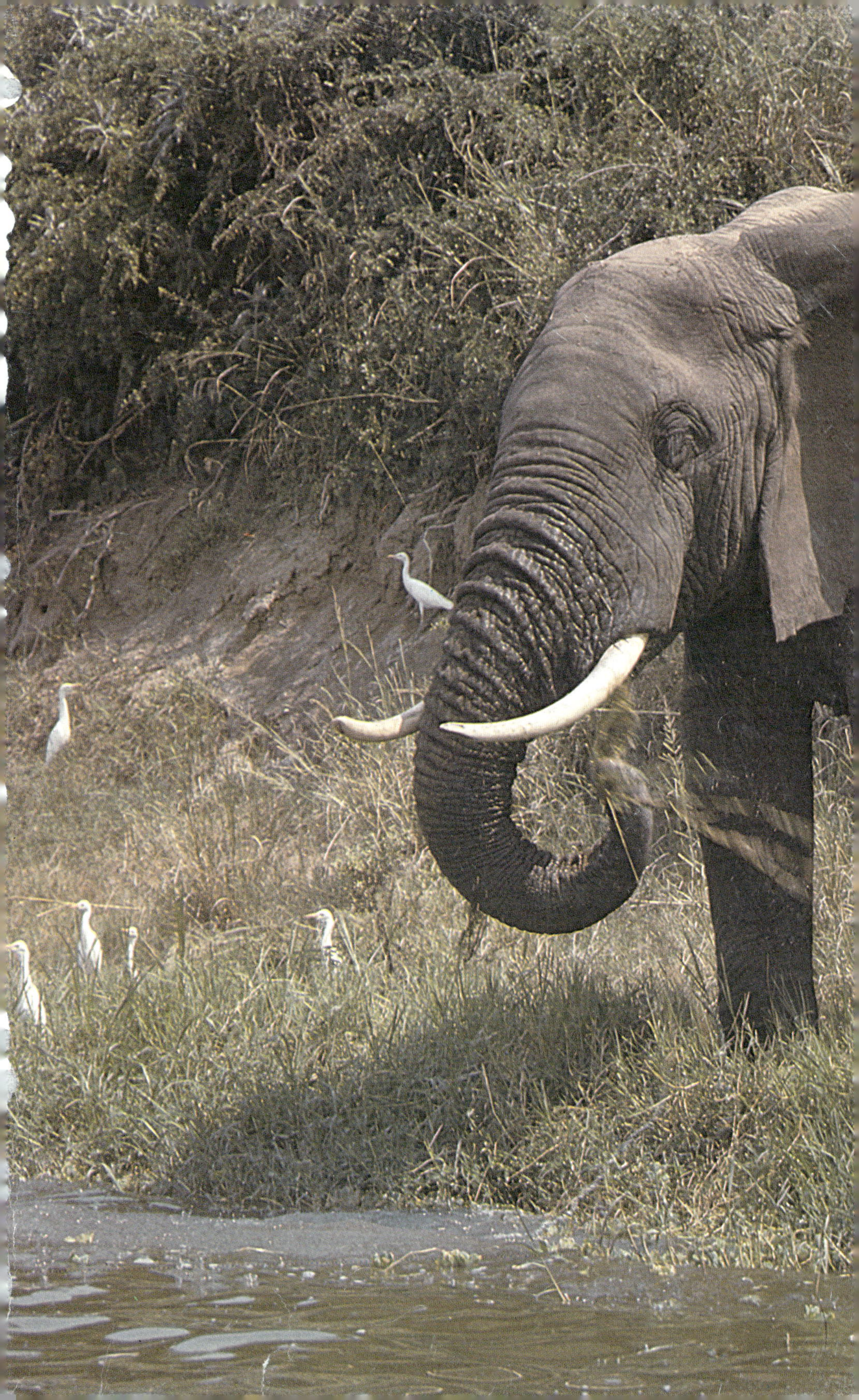

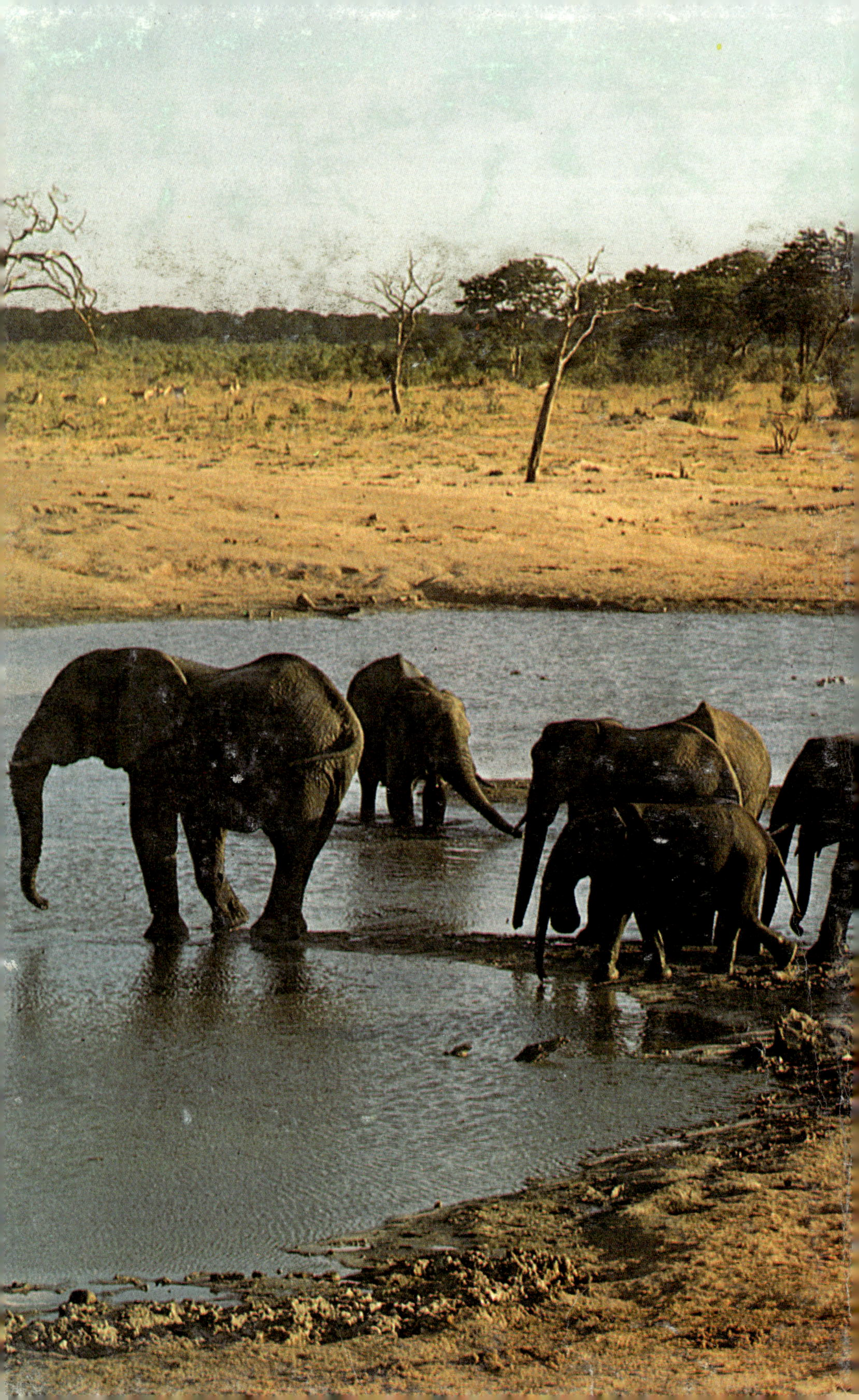

At the Water-hole

It is a hot day and
the elephants are drinking
at the water-hole.
They suck up the water
into their trunks and then
squirt it into their mouths.

This elephant is hot and itchy
so he is scratching himself
on a big rock.
Why do you think he is
flapping his ears?
(Answer on page 54)

Another elephant doesn't want to get wet so he kneels down to have a drink!
If the weather is very hot elephants don't have a bath because the water feels too cold.

▲
Here is an elephant
who doesn't want a bath.
The water is too cold so he squirts
mud all over himself instead.

These elephants are bathing.
Sometimes they help each other
to have a good bath.
The oldest elephants bath first
and the young ones wait until last.
▼

If the soil is red it makes
the elephant's skin red.
Some elephants are white.
Can you think why?
(Answer on page 55)

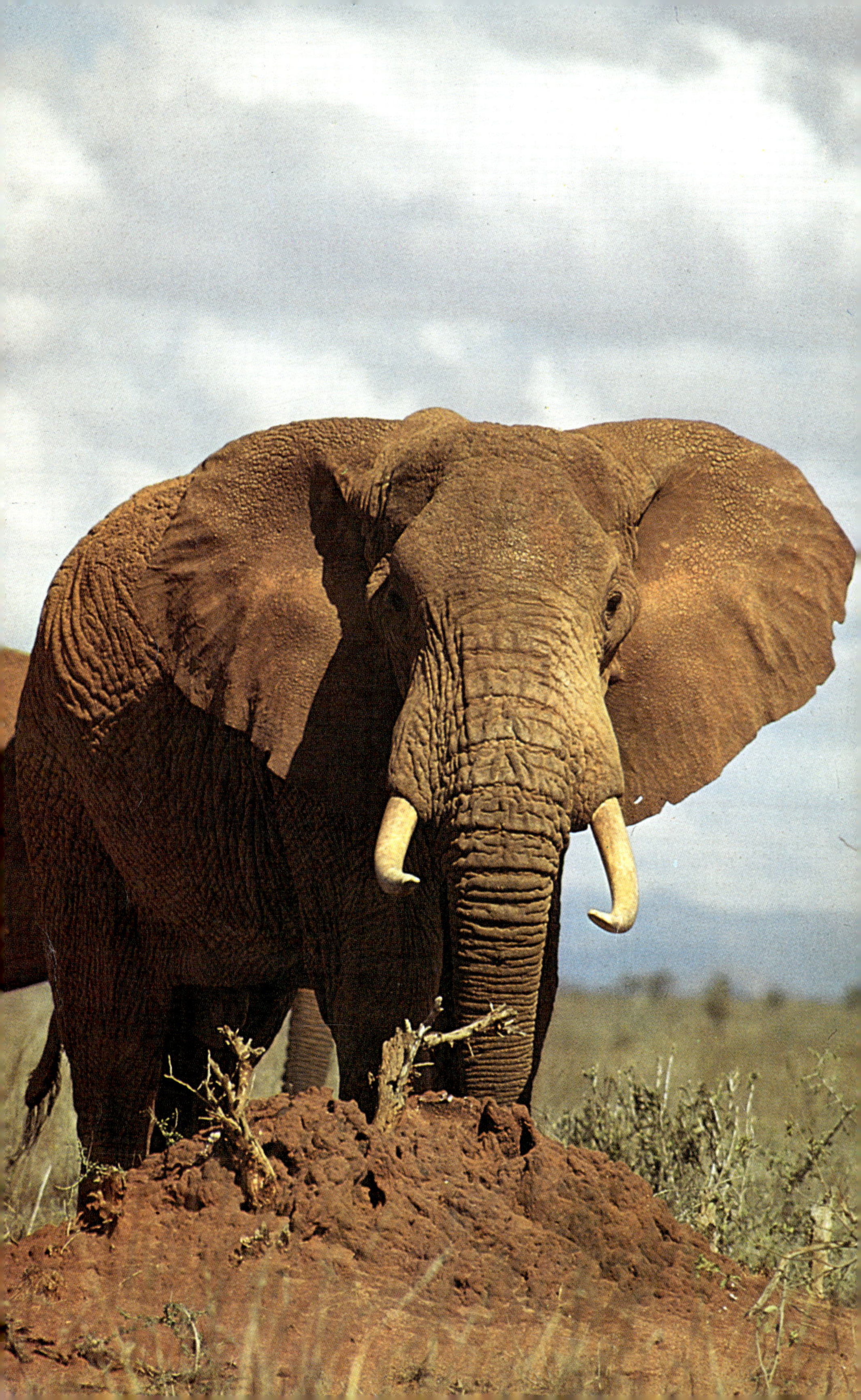

Here is a red elephant
looking for food.
Even his tusks are red
from digging in the red soil.

Elephants need water-holes because
they drink about 180 litres
(40 gallons) of water every day.

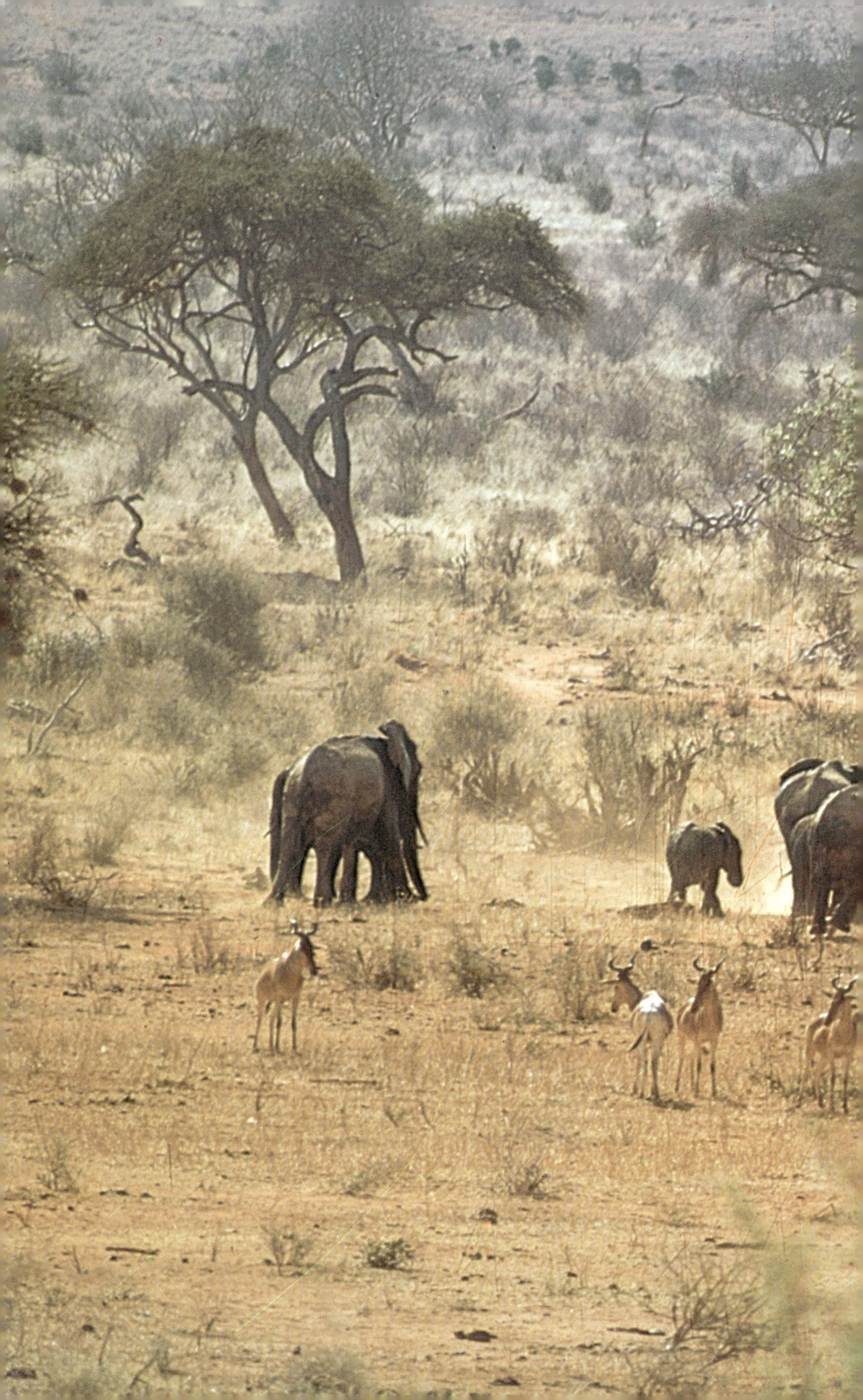

Moving On

These elephants are moving on
to another part of the bush.
The dried mud on their grey skins
is the same colour as the grass
and bushes around them.
You cannot see them easily but
they make plenty of noise!

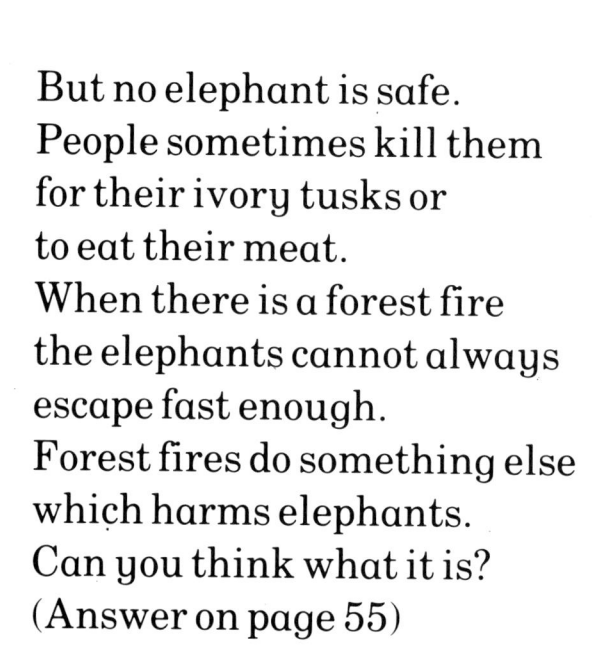

But no elephant is safe.
People sometimes kill them
for their ivory tusks or
to eat their meat.
When there is a forest fire
the elephants cannot always
escape fast enough.
Forest fires do something else
which harms elephants.
Can you think what it is?
(Answer on page 55)

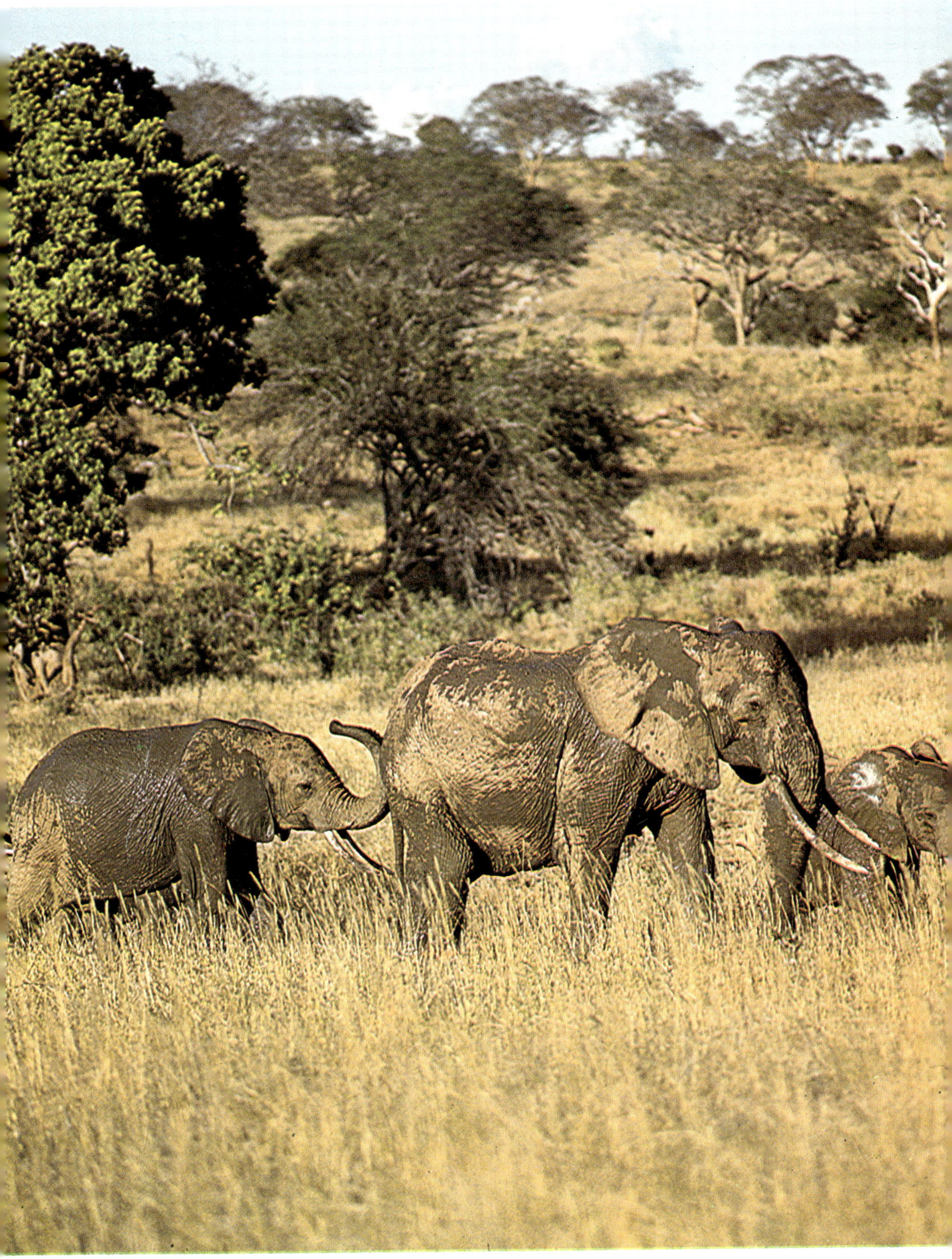

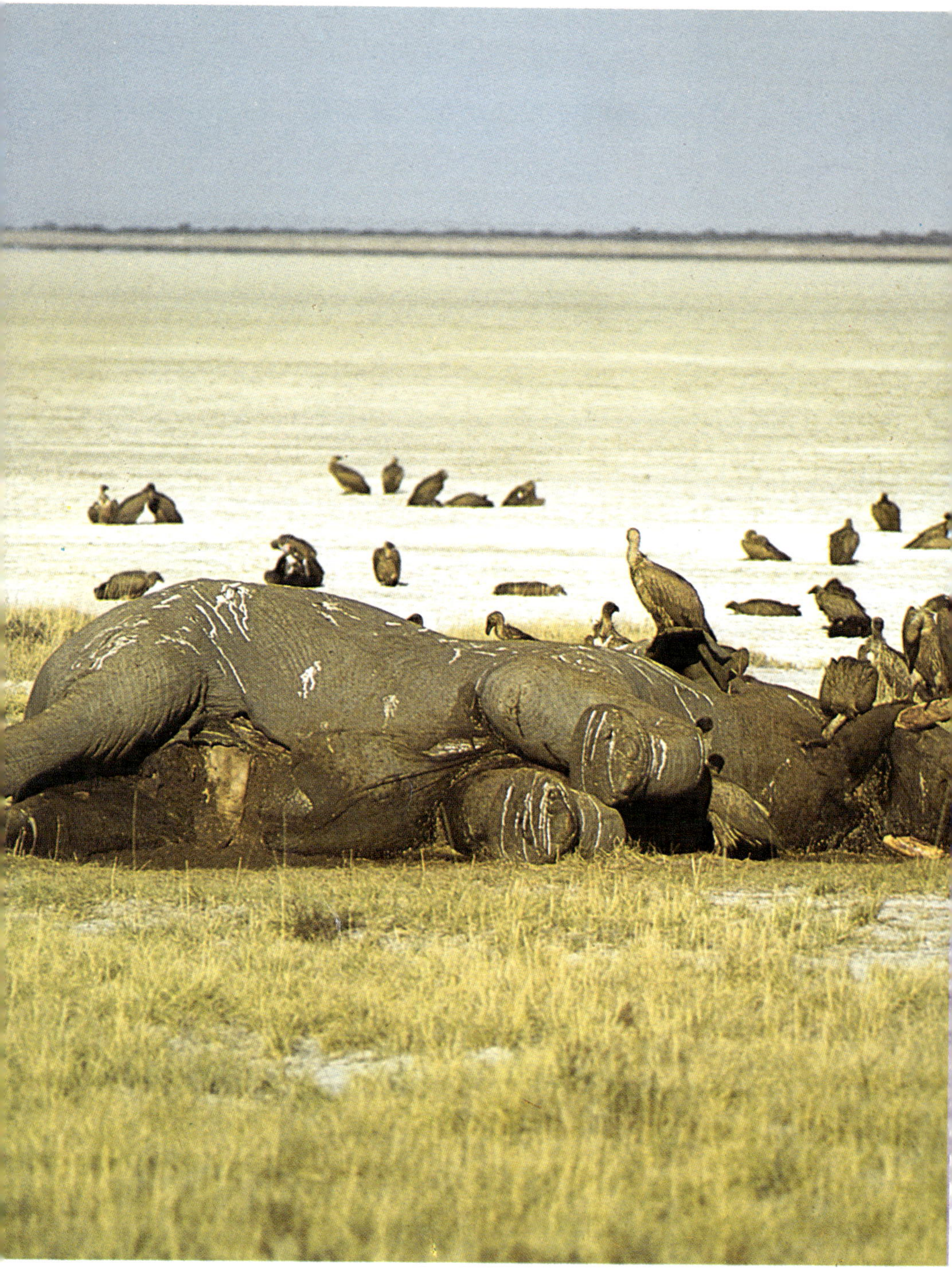

This elephant is dead and
the vultures will eat it.
Some elephants become ill and die.
Some elephants die of old age.
When they are old their teeth
wear out and they cannot eat
so they starve to death.

Elephants always look after each other.
When an elephant dies the others
touch it with their trunks.
Sometimes they cover its head
with sand and leaves.

How long do elephants live?
(Answer on page 55)

The elephants have walked
to a lake to drink
at the end of the day.

When it gets dark
they will go into the forest
to shelter for the night.

This elephant has a broken tusk.
Perhaps he had a fight
with another bull elephant.
It is harder for him
to tear the bark off the tree
but he will still have a good supper!

Is this elephant on fire?
No, he is having a dust bath.
He sucks the dust into his trunk
and blows it over his body.
The dust will clean his skin and
get rid of insects.

Now it is getting dark and
the elephants are going into the forest.

They will find a place
where they can sleep safely.

The elephants are asleep at last.
But they are standing up!
Elephants do not lie down
when they go to sleep and
no one knows why.

The elephants have had a long day.
They have eaten tree bark,
leaves and plants.
They have drunk water at the river,
the water-hole and the lake.
Some of them have had a bath.
Tomorrow they will set off again
to find fresh food and water
in the African bush.

How far do you think
elephants walk in a day?
(Answer on page 55)

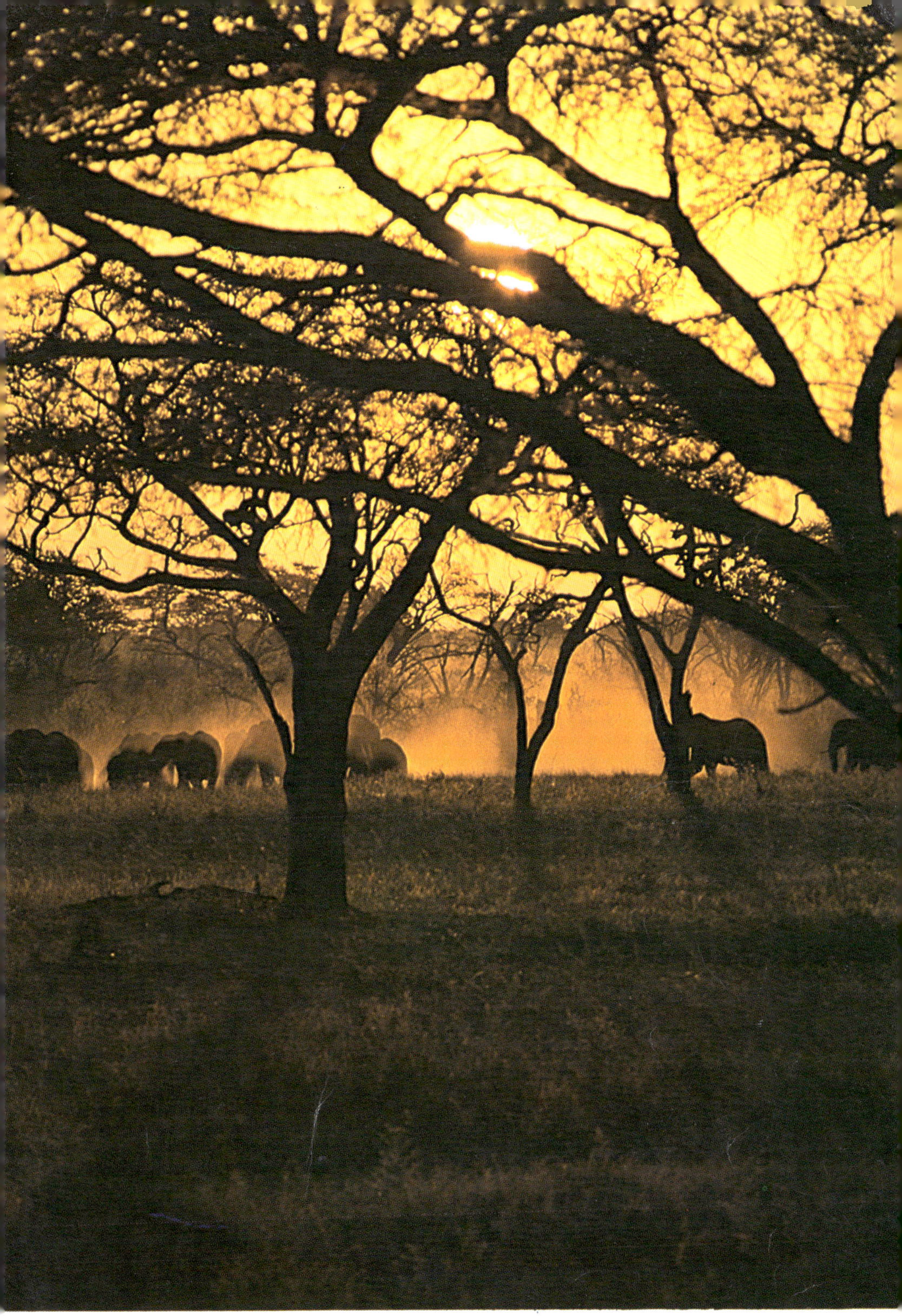

Answers to Questions

Page 8
Elephants have very thick skins
so that they can push through
forests and prickly bushes
without hurting themselves.

Page 17
The elephants have moved on
because they have eaten all the food.
They have to keep moving on
to find fresh food.

Page 28
The birds eat the insects
which make the elephants itch.

Page 33
The elephant is flapping his ears
like a fan to cool himself.

Page 37
Some elephants are white
because they live in places
where there is white dust.
The dust makes their skin white.

Page 42
Forest fires burn all the trees,
leaves, plants and berries
that elephants eat.

Page 45
Elephants can live up to 70 years
just like humans.

Page 52
Elephants walk between 10 and 15 km
(6–9 miles) every day.

Index

baby elephants 22, 24, 25, 27, 28
bathing 34, 35, 36, 52
birds 28, 54
bull elephants 22, 24, 48
charge 28
colours of elephants 37, 39, 42, 55
cow elephants 22, 24
death 45
drinking 13, 32, 34, 39, 46, 52
droppings 19
ears 28, 33, 54
eyes 7
fighting 23, 48
food 13, 14, 17, 18, 19, 25, 27, 39, 48, 52, 54, 55
forest fires 42, 55
herd 12, 16, 28
Indian elephants 8
insects 49, 54
lions 27, 28
mating 22, 24
mud 35, 42

noise 28, 42
size of elephants 5
sleep 51, 52
skin 8, 42, 49, 54, 55
teeth 6, 45
tigers 28
trees 14, 16, 17, 48, 52
trunk 8, 14, 27, 32, 45, 49
tusks 5, 6, 14, 23, 39, 42, 48
vultures 45
weight of elephants 5

Picture Acknowledgements
The illustrations in this book were supplied by: Ardea Photographics 6, 9, 14, 16, 17, 18, 19, 26, 32, 33, 34, 36, 37, 44, 48, 51, 53; Bruce Coleman *front cover*; Frank W. Lane 4, 7, 22, 27, 39; N.H.P.A. 12, 21, 23, 25, 29, 35, 49; Heather Angel *endpapers*, 41, 47; and Eric Hosking 11, 15, 31, 38 and 43.

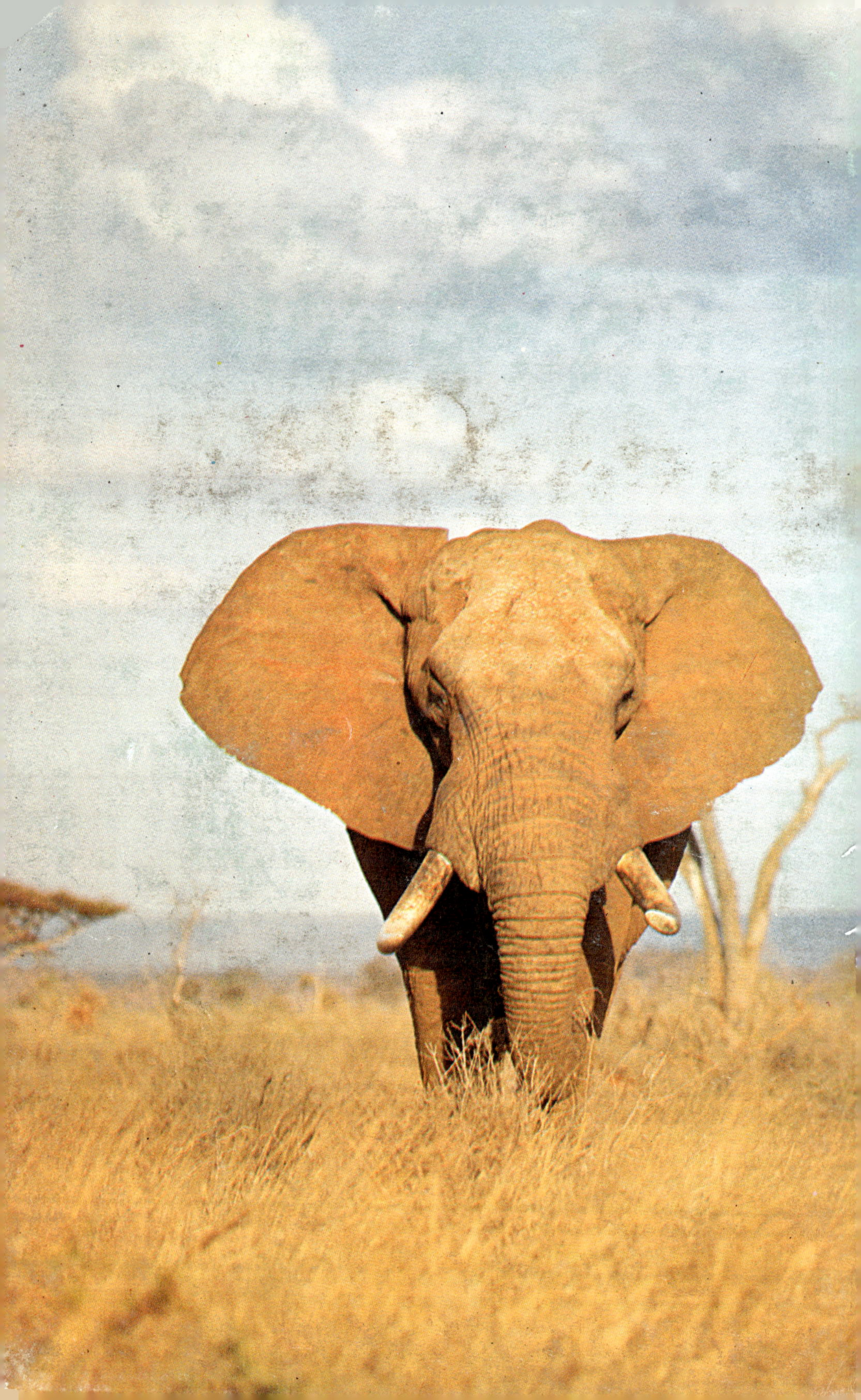